REALL y

USEFUL

VIOLIN DUETS!

WITH NOTE CHARTS

beginners

to

grade 3

written and arranged

by

Elizabeth Tebby Germaine ARCM

Published in 2015 by FeedARead.com Publishing

A CIP catalogue record for this title is available from the British Library.

INTRODUCTION

I have collected together the bits and pieces I carry around when teaching the violin. These arrangements and original duets make it easy for beginners to join in with something quickly, particular with folk music. At the same time they could be learning new notes, counting rests, trying unfamiliar time signatures, harder rhythms, new bowing techniques and other challenges.

Later they might find they had absorbed tunes and could play them by ear which is a useful skill to develop alongside other skills of note reading and building a good technique.

A complete beginner can fill in the open string notes in scales and arpeggios getting to know these patterns in advance.

Charts show note positions on the fingerboard and explain tones and semitones.

The folk tunes used here are written from memory or from scratch and may differ from similar tunes with the same or different titles. Most duets have no expression markings though some are most effective played fast or very fast. Ideas about speed and dynamics could be written in.

The duets can be played (or sung) on any treble instrument besides the violin.

CONTENTS
VIOLIN DUETS

OPEN STRINGS - EASY

OPEN STRINGS – MORE RHYTHMS

OPEN STRINGS – MORE BOWING

OPEN STRINGS – PLAY ALONG WITH...

OPEN STRINGS – C MAJOR

OPEN STRINGS – PIZZICATO

INCLUDING FINGER ONE

MORE FINGERS

BOWINGS AND RHYTHMS

INCLUDING CHROMATIC NOTES

HARMONICS

THREE FINAL DUETS

OPEN STRINGS - EASY

CLOWN DANCE

PATRICKS REEL

TALLIS CANON

JOIN IN WITH OLD MACDONALD IN D

SCALE AND ARPEGGIO OF A MAJOR

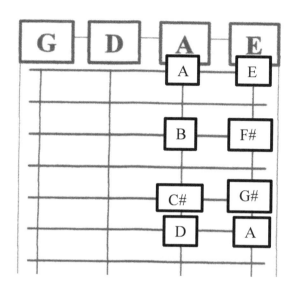

MISS MACLEOD'S REEL

TONES AND SEMITONES

SEMITONE = smallest distance between notes

| WHITE
BLACK
WHITE
BLACK |  | but
also
WHITE
WHITE |  |

BLACK NOTES HAVE TWO NAMES

| F# is also Gb | | C# is also Db |

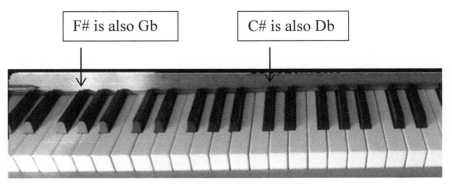

TONE = 2 SEMITONES

| WHITE
to
WHITE
G to A | also
WHITE
to
BLACK
B to C# | 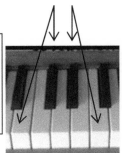 | and
BLACK
to
WHITE
Eb to F |

and
BLACK to BLACK
C# to D#

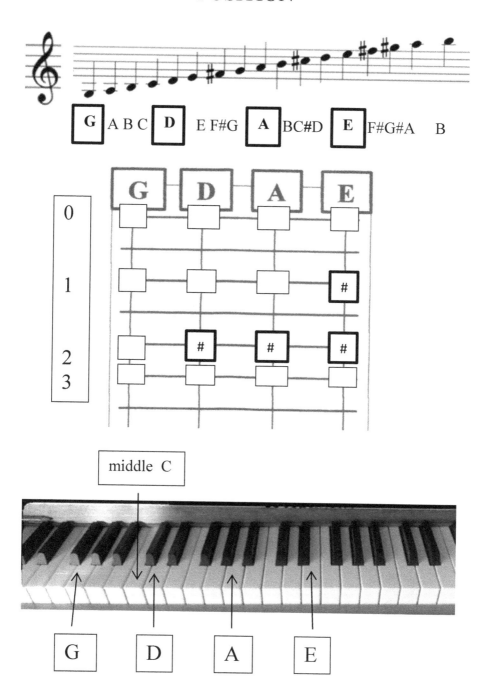

THE EASIEST VIOLIN NOTES IN FIRST POSITION

SCALE AND ARPEGGIO OF D MAJOR

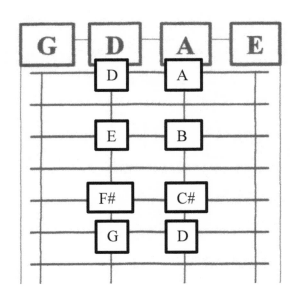

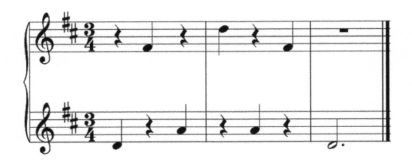

LET'S TALK

12

LET'S TALK AGAIN

13

JOIN IN WITH OLD MACDONALD IN G

SCALE AND ARPEGGIO OF G MAJOR

NOTE VALUES AND TIME SIGNATURES

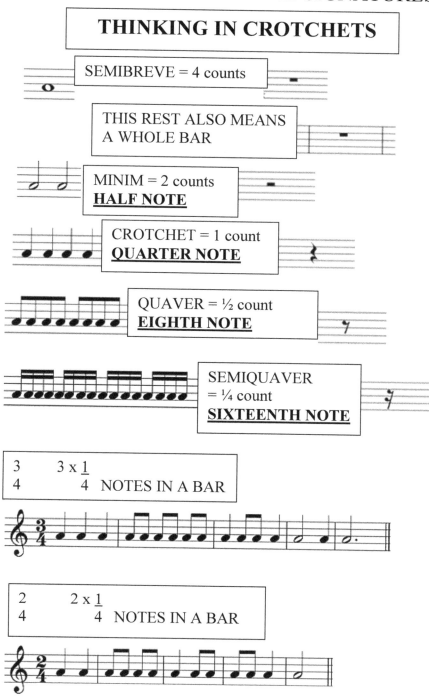

```
4        4 x 1
4            4   NOTES IN BAR
```

THINKING IN GROUPS OF 3 QUAVERS

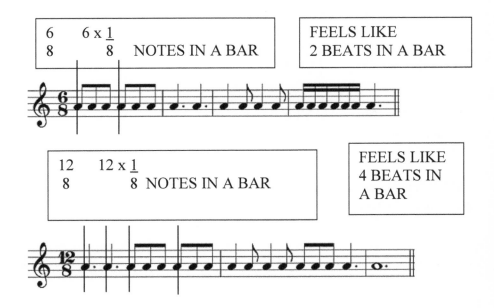

```
6        6 x 1
8            8   NOTES IN A BAR
```

FEELS LIKE
2 BEATS IN A BAR

```
12       12 x 1
8            8   NOTES IN A BAR
```

FEELS LIKE
4 BEATS IN
A BAR

THE DOT

THE DOT ADDS ON HALF OF THE NOTE IT FOLLOWS

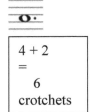

4 + 2
=
6
crotchets

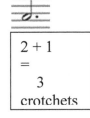

2 + 1
=
3
crotchets

1 + ½
=
1½
crotchets

½ + ¼
=
¾
of a crotchet

SOLDIERS' JOY

OPEN STRINGS
MORE RHYTHMS

THIS OLD MAN

SEMIQUAVERS

THE RAKES OF MALLOW

CATCH THE BUS!

22

very fast!   AN IRISH TUNE

2 beats in a bar

RUNNING

24

JAZZY

KEEP MOVING

OPEN STRINGS
MORE BOWING

SMOOTH CROSSING

29

$$\frac{2}{2} \quad 2 \times \frac{1}{2} \quad \text{NOTES IN A BAR}$$

LONG AND HEAVY

WALTZ WITH ME

LONG AND SHORT

OPEN STRINGS
PLAY ALONG WITH...

AULD LANG SYNE

HAPPY BIRTHDAY

SUPERCALIFRAGALISTICEXPIALADOCIOUS
(from the film Mary Poppins)

(Tune begins on F#)

AWAY IN A MANGER (in G)

(Tune begins on D)

THIS GOES WITH 'Consider yourself'
from 'Oliver'

Con | sider yourself | at | home! | Con

sider yourself | one of the | family ..... etc

(Tune begins on D)

OPEN STRINGS
C MAJOR

SCALE OF C MAJOR

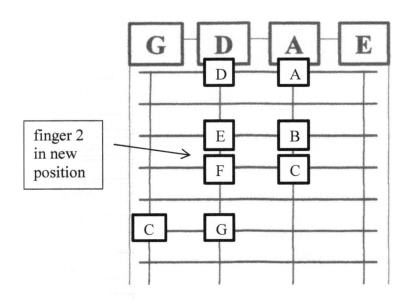

finger 2 in new position

ON THE KEYBOARD THIS IS THE EASIEST SCALE

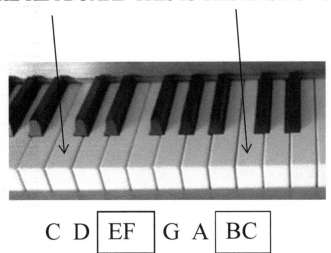

C D | EF | G A | BC |

37

the key
signature

JOIN IN WITH…
OLD MACDONALD IN C

38

SLOW PROCESSION

OPEN STRINGS
PIZZICATO

STRUMMING

INCLUDING FINGER 1

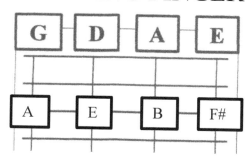

NOTE NAMES ON THE TREBLE CLEF

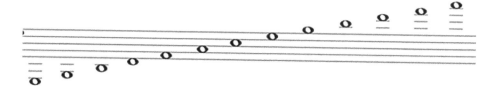

E	G	B	D	F	A	C	E	G	B	D	F	A

EVERY GOOD BOY DESERVES FISH AND CHIPS EVERY
GOOD BOY DESERVES FISH AND CHIPS EVERY

F	A	C	E	G	B	D	F	A	C	E	G

FISH AND CHIPS EVERY GOOD BOY DESERVES FISH
AND CHIPS EVERY GOOD

FINGERS FIRST SIX QUAVERS

43

STRANGE DREAM

KEEP BUSY

MORE FINGERS

SHARP SEMIQUAVERS

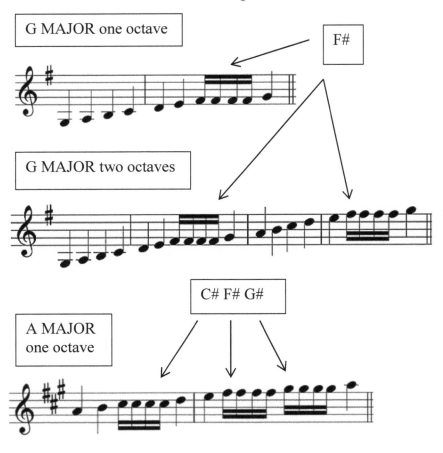

G MAJOR one octave

F#

G MAJOR two octaves

C# F# G#

A MAJOR
one octave

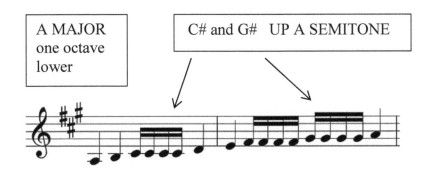

A MAJOR
one octave
lower

C# and G#   UP A SEMITONE

WALK THE DONKEYS

SCALE AND ARPEGGIO OF A MINOR (harmonic)

49

IN THE FOG

AT HOME

MARY'S BOY CHILD

THE COMPLETELY DIFFERENT
SCALE AND ARPEGGIO OF F MAJOR

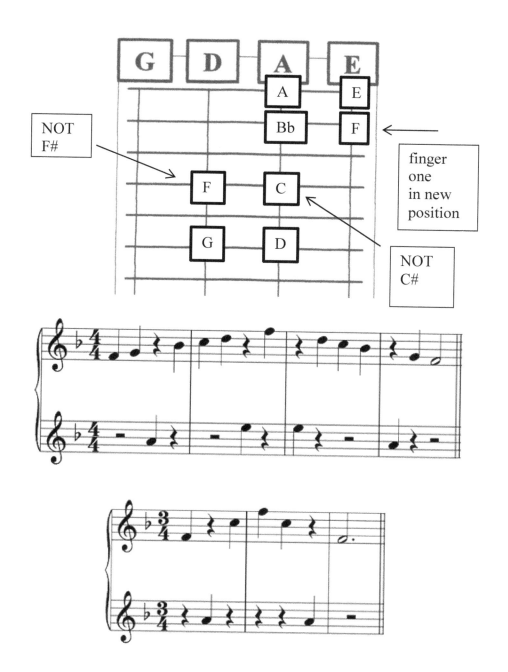

FOLK TUNE

BOWINGS
AND RHYTHMS

HURRY NOW HURRY NOW HURRY DOWN DOWN UP!

(This rhythm and bowing pattern is found in the short
extract from the William Tell Overture by Rossini set for
grade 2 ABRSM exams)

UP bows on
weak notes

strong notes (like
the first beat of the
bar) need DOWN
bows

UP BOW FIRST

58

SYNCOPATED

some notes fall BETWEEN the beats

INCLUDING
CHROMATIC NOTES

60

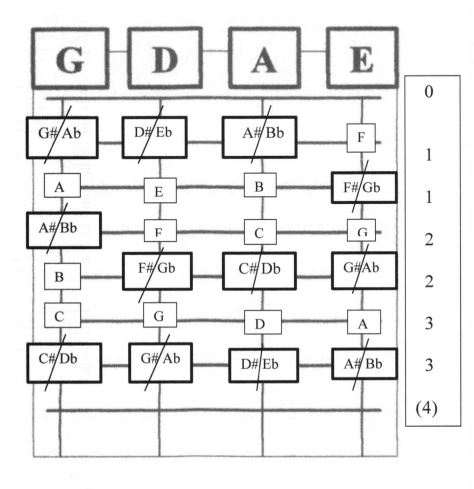

61

TWO VOICES

HEAVY

FOUR JAZZ

SCALE and ARPEGGIO OF Bb MAJOR

Eb /Bb new position finger 4

65

FAST FOLK

can go
very fast!

HARMONICS

all the notes in the
second part can be
played as harmonics
keeping hand in
4th position

THE SILVER MOON

shift the hand to find
the harmonics

MISS MACLEOD'S REEL

THREE FINAL DUETS

FLYING BOWS

fast bows will
help the fingers!

finger 2 on F natural and C natural

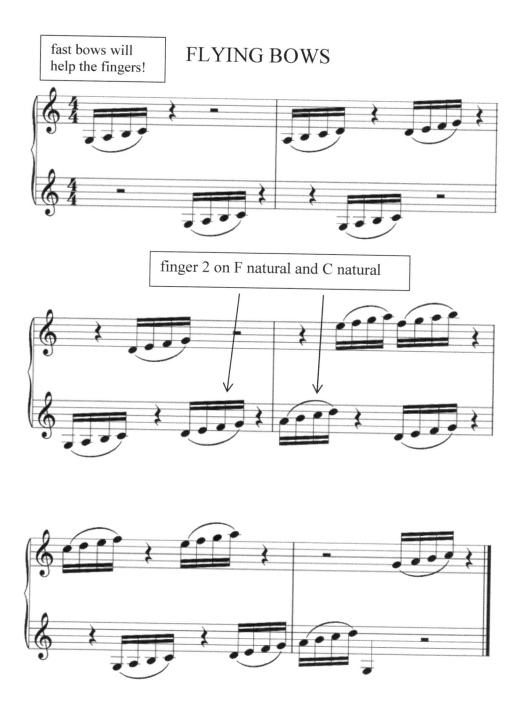

72

ON THE BRIGHT SIDE

big sound
long bows

GRAND FINALE

Other books by this author:

<u>MUSIC</u>

REALLY USEFUL NOTES!
a book for piano students grade 5-8
ISBN 978 17851 09812

<u>HISTORY</u>

DARK JUNGLE, STEEP MOUNTAINS
- refugee stories, Burma WW2
ISBN 978 1 78510 044 4

DISTANT AND DANGEROUS DAYS IN BURMA AND CHINA
- with stories of survival and many photographs
ISBN 978 1 78510 013 0